# Irregular Images

# More praise for *Irregular Images* & Edward Ahern's poetry

"Ed Ahern has given us a collection of one hundred poems. Read one or several each day and this volume will last a while. But some will last longer than awhile for they will stick with you like burrs you collect in your walks through the thickets of life."

Ray Rauth
Wilton Chapter Coordinator
Connecticut Poetry Society

"The themes of Ed Ahern's *Irregular Images* are nothing short of momentous—lust for life, transience, mortality. They are wrung through his short, quartz-hard poems with a force that sometimes attains to that of the Hopkinsian 'ooze of oil / Crushed.'

"A recurrent motif in Ed's work is the hunt, which, even as it pins the deer or the pheasant in the cross hairs, catches the poet himself in the lights, the frozen quarry within our larger viewing. Before long, we the readers are right there with him, hunters and hunted, ourselves swamped by the pervasive ache and terror of an impending blackout. Grim? Yes, but also immeasurably liberating."

Ralph Nazareth
Author of *Ferrying Secrets*
& co-author of *Dropping Death*

# Irregular Images

## EDWARD AHERN

Fairfield
SCRIBES

Copyright © 2019 Edward Ahern.

All rights reserved. This book or any portion thereof may not be reproduced or used in any manner whatsoever without the express written permission of the publisher, except in the case of brief quotations embodied in critical reviews and certain other noncommercial uses permitted by copyright law. For permission requests, write to the publisher at fairfield.scribes@gmail.com.

ISBN-13: 978-1-949122-10-7 (Paperback)
ISBN-13: 978-1-949122-11-4 (eBook)

Characters and events in this book are fictitious. Any similarity to real people, living or dead, is coincidental.

Cover photo courtesy of www.freerangestock.com
Other images courtesy of https://pixabay.com/—photographers credited when known.
Cover and interior design by Alison McBain.

Fairfield Scribes
Fairfield, CT
United States of America

First printing April 2019.

For the kind-hearted poets and listeners
who suffered through my first drafts.
You know who you are.

## ~ Contents ~

| | |
|---|---|
| The Explanation | 1 |
| Afterglow | 2 |
| Ebb Tide | 2 |
| Mystery Man | 3 |
| Facebook Findings | 4 |
| Shambling | 7 |
| Glancing Backward | 7 |
| The Church Service | 8 |
| My Father Time | 9 |
| Strewn Words | 11 |
| Vigils | 12 |
| Defining Veteran | 12 |
| Guilty Pleasures | 13 |
| By Default | 13 |
| Corporate Vision | 14 |
| Tombstone | 14 |
| Digger | 15 |
| Marking Time | 16 |
| Götterdämmerung | 16 |
| Bogeyman Dreams | 17 |
| Things | 18 |
| At the Cottage | 20 |
| Firelight | 22 |
| Biosphere | 23 |
| The Hunt | 25 |
| Dining Alone | 26 |
| Duel Desires | 27 |
| The Wake | 28 |

| | |
|---|---|
| The Fear Is in the Question | 30 |
| Hexen | 31 |
| Telling a Fortune | 32 |
| Luna Calls | 34 |
| Seasoning | 34 |
| Flying | 35 |
| The Relationship | 37 |
| The Flowers | 37 |
| The Storm Wind | 38 |
| Peace | 38 |
| The Layer Cake | 39 |
| Arrested Experiences | 40 |
| Traveling Light | 41 |
| The Urchin Response | 42 |
| The Snowstorm | 43 |
| Art in the Moment | 44 |
| Good Afternoon Death | 45 |
| Snow Melt | 45 |
| A Winter's Day | 47 |
| O'Leary's Drive-Thru | 48 |
| Boarders | 49 |
| In the Mood | 50 |
| Animal Eyes | 51 |
| Another Me | 52 |
| Progress | 53 |
| God's New Clothes | 54 |
| Take It All Off | 55 |
| Ice Out | 56 |
| Interlude | 56 |
| Keeping Company | 57 |
| Defining the Species | 58 |

| | |
|---|---|
| The Shoal | 60 |
| The Deer Chase | 62 |
| Careful Wonder | 63 |
| The Game | 64 |
| Damn Dog Died | 64 |
| The Yard Party | 65 |
| Taking a Pheasant | 66 |
| Revisitations | 68 |
| The Adoration | 69 |
| Rock Piles | 70 |
| The Charter Boats | 73 |
| Rules | 74 |
| Being Ignored | 74 |
| Storm Tossed | 75 |
| Leaf Fall | 75 |
| Fellow Traveler | 76 |
| Noel | 77 |
| Resolutions | 77 |
| An Apology for Hate | 78 |
| Stirrings | 79 |
| Trapped Under the Yule Log | 79 |
| The Dog Walk | 80 |
| The Name Cascade | 81 |
| Falling Away | 82 |
| Solitary Nocturne | 83 |
| The Swamp Oak | 85 |
| A Movement in the Shadows | 86 |
| Commiserating Poetry Month | 87 |
| The Crone Zone | 87 |
| Fright of Passage | 88 |
| A Measure of Man | 89 |

| | |
|---|---|
| Currents | 90 |
| Bedtime Story | 91 |
| The Alms of Strangers | 92 |
| Seasonal Lament | 95 |
| Chance Encounters | 95 |
| The Sparrow Nest | 96 |
| The Predators | 97 |
| The Wayfarer | 98 |
| Firelight | 99 |
| Legacy | 101 |
| About the Poet | 105 |

# The Explanation*

Dear Grandchildren,
You may remember on occasion
That I wrote stories and poems.
And you may even, on a slow day,
Read one and wonder
Why the hell I did it.
So here's the A to Z of why I wrote.
I liked to expose myself.
Not literally of course.
I was too old to make it interesting.
But just in images that give you
Acquaintance with my distended views
Of our existence.

**\* a pangram**

# Afterglow

In the blurred pastel focus of my dotage, my wrongs and excesses are landmarks, not of evil, but of what I thought I could enjoy without retribution. The good I've done, and there has been much of it, compresses like the retirement home grass I step on to reach for the vivid nettles of roguery growing just outside my fenced-in state. My memories of vice are so much more poignant than those of virtue.

# Ebb Tide

Sometimes my low tides drop me
onto rocks and sharp edges.
coated with the seaweed rot
of decomposing failures
and littered with the broken shells
of promises unkept.
But in time, always,
the flood tide surges
washing clean my feet
and carrying me onward.

# Mystery Man

Listen closely to a woman
and she'll tell you who she is.
Listen closely to a man
and he'll tell you who he pretends to be.
A man plays a game of I hide, don't seek
and plays it well.
His script is memorized.
and reassuring.
Banalities to associates
and excuses without fault.
But a man does not deceive himself
and will tell his mutilated truths.
But only to another man
and only when greatly threatened.
Women rarely reach beyond the image
To the hidden in their men.

# Facebook Findings*

Press and like the number five.
Jane the virgin on Twitter
This spoon takes away
the effects of the shakes

When you get fresh sheets
and you just shaved your legs.

This dude spent eight years
growing a chair
Shannon has exactly 200 friends.
Kakistocracy—government by
the worst available people.

You are convicted by your complicity.
Did Jesus leave us a tip to diabetes?
This is what happens when
you wrap your teeth in
aluminum foil for an hour.

Age your spirits at home.

There are several islands
atop the falls
and they are Zambian.

There's a lot of gross bullshit
that goes on
in the creative world.

Please like and share.

**\* found poem**

Photo credit: Didier Aires

## Shambling

In the humble jumble of my life
I plumb stumble
With grumbles and mumbles
Through tumbles and bumbles
And numb fumbles
As my life, with a rumble, crumbles.

## Glancing Backward

The just-happened riffles away from me.
Dwindling into distant truths and shrunken lies.
Unrecorded, most-valued moments
Roiling with the inconsequential into
Dirty, brown froth.
The who I was drowned in misremembering
Leaving only debris on the surface.

# The Church Service

In between singing and praying
and chanting and preaching
is silence.
And in that stillness we overhear
the rustling of demons uncomfortable
in hypocrisy.
Under the fancy-dressed pieties
are the soiled linens of
our weaknesses
that we fear or relish repeating,
that infiltrate our thoughts even
while praying.
The evils of our being writhe
unearthed on the bare soil of
our devotion.

# My Father Time

My father died when I was ten
in a motel bathroom in Texas.
Heart attack wrote the doctor.
War shrapnel insisted my mother.
He was thirty-eight.

He traveled for his job,
and spent evenings in a bar
with his friends.
I remember him fondly,
but not well.

I believe he loved me,
but cannot remember a hug,
I knew his kindness
but never got to know him,
and never will.

# **Strewn Words**

There is a fertile recess in my being
that shelters weedy thoughts
and emotions without edging,
and so long as I allow myself
to sense without pruning
and think without word killer
poetry will grow.

In their shelters swarms of poets
clutch handfuls of seed phrases,
hybrids of deviant visions,
and strew them in near blindness
in hope that a few will settle
inside other mind arbors
and germinate a second sight.

## Vigils

Faces blur, dates are forgotten,
and stories grow fabulous,
but names abide, and feelings.

Emotions hold true
about those who were,
about their absence.

Memories flicker
and decorate our beings
like votive lights.

## Defining Veteran

My ship was melted into razor blades decades ago.
Shipmates have moved on and perhaps left life behind.
What I remember is probably not quite true,
But I still define who I am
By what I was and did.
By how I served.

# Guilty Pleasures

Evil is more complex than good.
My memories still half-alive
are of things that shouldn't be done,
and my waking delusions
are preoccupied with seven things deadly.

Omnipresent talk and acts
tell me I'm not abnormal,
but I survive best
with an active imagination
that replaces acting out.

# By Default

A life is not things chosen,
it is the things declined.
The paths not trod,
the partners not pursued,
the help not given,
the toil not done.
A life is burnt in by omissions
whose only traces are ash.

## Corporate Vision

I was corporate not once but twice,
pledging loyalty and dedication
as I should.
But more was required.
With the handshake swearing in
I became beholden to
intransigent practices
and firmly skewed outlooks.
My words self-filtered,
my principles in refuge,
the required lie unspoken
but ponderous.

## Tombstone

Why are you reading this stone apology
for someone you cannot further know?
What I am does not linger under the granite.
What we were no longer grows.
Our dried flowers of shared affection
will crumble if grasped at.
Just glance at us from time to time.

# Digger

We called him Digger
because when he wasn't too drunk
he dug graves.

We called him Digger
because he thought poorly
and a dog's name seemed apt.

We called him Digger
because we needed to isolate
his sickness from our own.

We called him Digger
because he smiled as
his addiction betrayed him.

We called him Digger
because our help
failed each time.

We called him Digger
because when he went missing
we didn't remember his name.

# Marking Time

Two-legged beings,
floating until birth,
bed-bound for sleep,
legless for eating and work,
prone again for sex,
littered for sickness,
kneeling for defeat,
death-bedded for departure.
And in between
standing around
marking time.

# Götterdämmerung

Vampire paramours but vanished brides of Christ.
Allah as warmonger but warlocks as heroes.
Fashionable witches but forgotten saints.
Buddha as bracelet charm but beloved murderers.

Peculiar
To abandon Gods
And fixate on monsters.

# Bogeyman Dreams

As a child and young adult
my dreams sometimes writhed
with beings who lusted after
my powerless body or soul
and I faced the morning's rise
with shuddering relief.

Such dreams have deserted me.
The nightmare panic that bound me
in delicious fear is gone.
I am shriveled by the lack,
for more than any wish fulfillment
they assured me I was alive.

My worst dreams are now annoyance
that I am detoured from achieving
my trifling unconscious ambitions,
cloying moebius loops of frustration.
If the Bogeyman were to dream
he would have nightmares such as these.

# Things

Our clothes tatter, our shoes smell,
our wood decays, our paper brittles,
our marble chips, our silver tarnishes,
our drives corrupt, our food rots,
our steel rusts, our wine sours.
Flawed and failed.

Some things are nice, some necessary
Some liked, some lusted after
Some longer lived, some longer liked.
Some adored, some abused,
Some displayed, some defaced.
Donated and discarded

Yet some things of no value
are close, are comfort,
are talismans, are touchstones,
are emblems, are ensigns,
are memorials, are monuments.
Kindred and kept.

These we will not part with,
these we have no buyers for,
these we touch with reverence,
these we hide from other eyes,
these we see ourselves in.
Honored and haunted.

A bronze medallion faces me,
a fat man perched on sacks,
a god of prosperity,
a promise of well-being,
a wish in my decline.
Tarnished and treasured.

The scuffed wallet rests in my drawer,
the lone dollar enfolded.
His estate
the day he killed himself.
The leather urn holds friendship,
lost but lingering.

# At the Cottage*

There was no measure of the day at the cottage.
Water rustled over glacier rocks along the shore
The sound soft or loud at the whim of the waves
The rhythm slower with bigger swells from the lake
The iron water glistening the multicolored stones
That our pausing to admire drew mosquitos.

The rent we paid was the blood we gave to mosquitos
So we could see gray-painted dusk at the cottage
With blues and greens wiped from the face of the lake.
The forest kept its silence so the waves
Could play the instruments along the shore
And let us hear the personalities of the stones.

Some made from death, some made from fire, the stones
Sheltered life but turned away mosquitos
Who could not breed in moving water at the cottage.
And were driven into the forest by the waves
That protected only their own within the lake.
And guarded against the land along the shore.

The trees tendrilled close to ice outs along the shore
And root-cuddled until they could split the stones
And give the water pockets to the mosquitos
The woods bunched thick behind the cottage
Deadfall and live growth muffling the sound of waves
And spurning any memory of lake.

As cold June nights wedded the chills of the lake.
The unseen sounds came closer from along the shore
And from the woods the hidden hum of mosquitos
Was static in the music of the stones
That shifted and played in front of the cottage
In time with the dulcet beating of the waves.

Even in pauses of calm, tiny waves
Snuck outward from a waveless lake
And pattered like ferret feet along the shore.
And stirring in their sleep, the stones
Made less noise than the windless mosquitos.
Who feasted on us at the cottage.

Stones still creep from depth to decorate the shore
And waves write memoirs about the moody lake
And children of my mosquitos wait for me at the cottage.

**\* a sestina**

# Firelight

The allure of an open fire,
warmth aside,
is an inarticulate wish
for pyromancy,
for the flames to reveal
in flickers
the whys and wherefores
of living.
Thoughts swirl in updrafts,
grasping for
the random patterns,
tantalized
by closeness to ineffable
substance.

# Biosphere

Animals rarely creep inside my space
And rarer still are found and put to flight
Yet grackles pecked to nest inside my place
And spiders drop upon my head at night.
In Canada a hundred baby mice
emerged from walls to scurry past my feet
Not caring they disturbed a paradise,
Too busy fleeing rats to climb my sheets.
I shoo all vagrants out or squish them flat,
but those unseen are left to rest unsought.
The skunk beneath the stoop has gone to fat.
The gutters hold the squirrels still unfought.
Our game is just a little hide no seek
And residence is granted only to the meek.

Photo credit: Thilo Becker

# The Hunt

To hunt well is to kill,
cleanly or after wounding.
Motives are incidental,
food, sport, trophies.
The art requires a death.

There is pleasure
in a skilled tracking or ambush
only if successful,
a sense of survival competence
in powerless existence.

Method is incidental,
bow or gun or snare.
Difficulty is welcomed,
aching, chilled muscles,
strained in carcass dragging.

To seek prey
is to cherish closure,
abandoning flabby conventions
and trekking into finality.
To hunt well is to kill.

# Dining Alone

There is a moment in a solitary meal
when I'm bored with my thoughts
and the waitress has deserted me.
The food is bland and the mind is hungry.
I stretch my listening like sucker vines
to close-set tables with spoken words,
and take a seat at their conversations
so I can share moods and judge lives
by what's said over mashed potatoes.

An old couple exchange quiet insults
that they've repeated for decades,
no defense necessary or expected.

The software trainees talk mods and gaming,
clothing themselves in just-learned jargon,
while struggling to program their lives.

The young couple, not sure
if they're with the right person,
awkwardly skate on slippery banalities.

And I retreat to my own thoughts
more comfortable in lonely doldrum
than in communal malaise.

# Duel Desires*

The enemy of love is boredom.
The nurture of lust is wonder.
Daily caresses become pats.
Accessible secrets beckon.
Adoration calcifies into affection.
The almost-touched creates a tingle.
Soft words froth into foam.
Whispered words resonate.
Comforting pleasures enfold doubt.
Dangling passions are plucked.

**\*contrapuntal**

# The Wake

There you are at last,
On the far side of the kneeler.
Finely dressed as always,
Poker-faced as ever.
There's so much I need to tell you.

I know you got her pregnant,
And made me grow a stranger.
I know you bribed our clients
And sold their loyalty off.
I know you lied and stole.

And I held my silence.
For her sake.
For the business.
For your ever-breeding wife.
For my pathetic image.

But here you are at last,
Plump and pasty,
Dead to me now.
Oblivious of the wrongs,
Uncaring of the hurts.

No, don't stand up yet.
Hold that bogus sadness
Just a few seconds more
While I savor the thought
Of watching your arrival.

# The Fear Is in the Question

Some fear is belly-rotting:
>Will I be arrested?
>Am I being fired?

Some fear is nerve-searing:
>Is she alive?
>Is he leaving me?

Some dwarf fear is blood-pounding:
>Will I always be ugly?
>Where will I find the money?

But the fear that is mind-roaring,
The worst fear, is not:
>Am I dying?

But:
>What have I become?

# Hexen

We are dark arts predators
culling from God's herd,
tormenting his blameless,
hurling yin curses at his yang.

And we in turn are prey
for his rapacious holy
our master maims with equal ease
through God's harshly pious.

But spare your feeble pity
for the Hexen you may meet,
you are merely sacrifice
for the good of evil.

# Telling a Fortune

Come in, my dear, and sit in that chair.
What's that? No, no crystal ball, no incense.
Just a table and two chairs, and you and I.
Before you pay me, I must give you a choice.
Choose between two fortunes—neither of them lies.

One lets you look in a mirror,
What you will do, who you will bed,
The future as others are able to see you.
Most are content with that.

The other? Ah, that's much more painful.
I will flay your image and look inside you
At what you become and what you fail to be.
Your essence as it purifies or taints.

Most are unhappy with these revelations,
But recognize their truth
Even though they rarely change.
So what will it be?

Inner or outer, the money is the same.
My actions will not vary.
But I will be looking at you
Either dressed up or naked.

The procedure? Absurdly simple.
Your elbow on the table, fingers straight out.
I set my hands on each side of yours
And pass them up and down, just not touching.

Your hand feels pressure and warmth.
Both are phantoms, but not unreal.
Your focus is through your hand
As I begin to know you.

I ask no questions, that would be fraud.
Only begin to tell you
Of what you will have done
Or what you will become.

What's that? No, of course I understand.
Most people prefer to know
The course of their life rather than
The curses of their nature. Shall we begin?

## Luna Calls

A madwoman pleaded for help
From the shambles of her life.
But the help was for her madness,
Affirming evil that never was.
My sympathy nourished delusion.
My silence rejected need.
After caring but meaningless phrases
I threw her the sanely real,
Alms that left her in the brambles of her mind.

## Seasoning

Over the years
Several women drew close,
Differing in marvelous ways.
But all, early on or later in the time together,
Were pushed away or saw enough to leave.
Remembered in swirls of abiding fondness.
Piquant almosts sprinkled on a bland existence.

# Flying

Once, seeming not long ago
I dreamed of flying.
Racing without resistance
Along shore cliffs and over chasms.
Brushed by tree-top branches and skyscraper flags.
Gently indifferent to the surface bustle.

But with hair and deeper voice
Came weight
and fear of falling.
And more timid man-high risings
That let others pull me down.
Until I could not soar at all.

My dreams for decades
Have never been of flight,
And I am not unhappy, roped to earth.
But only hope
That my decline will free me
With an infant's tentative movement
To play again in the sky.

Photo credit: Antonio Doumas

## The Relationship

I can only think of you
with exasperation
at the challenging mix
of slick and stinging ways
that make you
my cactus.

## The Flowers

It's not the fault of flowers.
They were contented weeds.
Till pulled and stuck in bower
And bred to suit one's needs.
A weed is wild and never cowers.
A flower is cut for greed.
A flower is sent for lack of word.
A weed is plucked as loving deed.
As tarty, smelly petals sour
Give weeds their hour to feed
And all the beds devour.

# The Storm Wind

gusts and surges
like an unchained guard dog,
strewing dust and pollen,
flashing the naked underside
of leaves,
and tossing meadow grass
like ruffled bear fur,
spinning from side to side
in drunken dance,
a rioting brawl that cannot last,
and ends
with a watery flourish of thunder.

# Peace

Peace comes dropping slow
Like the drips after a rainstorm.
Not in the event, but in its departure.
Not in the emotion, but in its afterglow.
Peace is the pensive echo of tumult,
And self-awareness that it must pass.
Peace comes dropping slow.

# The Layer Cake

We are a skewed birthday cake,
generations of lopsided layers
baked badly by ancestors
of fervent but defective intent,
teetering atop the stale and dried out.

The layers descend into the past,
inedible and mostly forgotten
while we the temporary top deny
bad ingredients and tiltings
and frosting with crème cruel.

We concoct the next tier
with hope and even love
but use a cookbook specifying
flour of custom and bias
and spices of mistakes.

It is a mighty wonder
that the cake still stacks
and those just set in place
don't slide off to extinction
on the icing of our failings.

# Arrested Experiences

There's a border to experience that I have no urge to cross,
pained and severed living that I never want to know,
a suffering of friends that I hope not to feel.

They speak coded words of what's been undergone,
of copping, and outstandings, and going away,
of throwaway jobs, or hard time, or having to be a player.

They stare to one side and speak in flat tones
of beggars' freedom without family or belongings,
of bleak nows and worse futures and the urge to score.

I hope to never know the pain that shows
in their tattered voices and somber faces,
but venerate their ability to withstand it.

# Traveling Light

As I try to explore a lifetime
I keep gathering in trinkets and toys
that festoon me like a porcupine
bristling with impediments,
and glaze over my vision
with the tastes of others.
These consumptive accretions
Horse-collar my attention into
dragging along the already passé.

There is no thing I would risk death for
and yet I squander life on new burdens;
a caricature of free will,
a lead-winged bird,
an object lesson for nimbleness lost,
moving too ponderously to explore.

# The Urchin Response

Polar North Estates
25 Reindeer Stable
Nunavut, Canada


Dear _____,*

Thank you for your scribbled indecipherables. Please be advised that illegible requests receive default presents at management discretion. Said presents may be of a value significantly less than the original puerile demand.

Management takes no responsibility for coal lumps broken in transit.

*Not responsible for letters mis-sent to smudged addresses.*

# The Snowstorm

The wind shoves the flakes downward,
a falling, frozen cloud that seals
the man-made lawns and walks
beneath howling, formless anarchy.

The road unplowed, the car buried,
poor-me chatter bouncing across the screen.
There is little that would induce me
to burrow out and slew my way from home.

Loss of power, truly close friend, hunger.
My world, after all, is small.

# Art in the Moment

Tweets and blogs and selfies,
cuttings and transplants and mascara:
beloved embalming agents.
This moment is insufficient
to linger for save-my-now
who flash-freeze the transient.

Yet no day knows its father
and passion hovers but does not abide.
Our essences are painted on water,
and blown away like clouds.
But we take such pains
to enshrine images of who we no longer are.

## Good Afternoon Death

I cannot force myself to fear
a pleasant, sunny day,
and yet that's when
most people kill people.
Road rage, gang fights, bank robbery
Car wrecks, drug deals, spousal slayings
Suicides and matricides and random death.

I cannot force myself to enjoy
a dank and gloomy night
and yet I'm safer with the monsters.

## Snow Melt

My snow takes form and color
As it drains away.
Young powder clotting into abstracts.
Tanned gray by sky-fall earth.
No longer timeless, its weathered character
Ever changes, never lingers.

# A Winter's Day

When snow's gone dead with cold
And makes a brittle crunch
When air's a choking slush
That sears the lungs to suck
When fingers touch a frozen mouth
That cannot speak of feeling
Then winter's squatted frigidly
On all the open ground
And driven off with frost-bit whips
All those who live by warmth
Yet thought they owned the world

# O'Leary's Drive-Thru

The sign at the entrance ramp
explains it all.
Welcome to O'Leary's Underway Wakes.
Please tune your entertainment system
to www.dearlydeparted.doom.
Please select a dead person
from the drop-down menu.
Text condolences to the number shown.
Donations for eflowers, more eco-friendly
than floral arrangements, can be made
using your cell phone.
Corpse viewing at 5 mph.
A second drive-thru is available
at no additional cost.
Enjoy!

# Boarders

When was it
That we quit killing animals
And they opted to move back.
Neighborhoods teeming with humans
Are somehow settled by
Squirrels and possums and skunks
Song birds and crows and ducks
Raccoons and chipmunks and mice
Blue jays and woodpeckers and grackles
Deer and rats and feral cats
All visited by coyotes.
Surprising amount of room at the inn.

# In the Mood

In the thunder weather of my conscious
anvil ego clouds sprawl and bluster
over cotton puffs of moral fluster.

And ragged anger flashes down
with almost no illumination,
just jagged spikes of irritation.

This churning mood I know will slack,
leaving me with sodden friends
and the acrid ozone of amends.

# Animal Eyes*

Are we less or more human
When we watch the world
Through animal eyes?

When we react to strangers
Through the growls or purrs
Of the four-legged?

When we ensure that
The hair-lined mammal
Is fed before us?

Do we bond with fellow men
Based on association with dogs
Or cohabitation with cats?

Are we subspecies hominids
Living for the company
Of the inarticulate?

Probably.

But I have spent forty years
Observing life through animals' eyes
And feel better for it.


**\*For Barbara the catwoman.**

# Another Me

I carry another life with me.
Not spouse or child,
they walk on their own.
A conception of my devising,
an entity of should and must,
an avatar of the required
who exists in my stead.

Just once I tried
to throw him off,
to slash his webbing,
to be genesis of myself.
But the other clung
and tangled my intentions
and the moment passed
and he again enveloped me.
I carry another
On a path I would have forsaken.

And I wonder
in the quiet times
who I would be
having cast myself asunder.

# Progress

We were children of Seb* the earth god.
Born of soil arid or fertile,
becoming what we lived on.
But as Millenia turned we flinched
away from grounded life,
onto tiers of concrete and asphalt,
clambering into ersatz rooting
until we were nurtured,
not by earth but by artifice.


And when what we were starved
we ate what Shu* provided
from the doctored air we lived in
hoping that he did not become
his aspect of punishment
who would kill off our corruption.


**\* Egyptian gods**

# God's New Clothes

So little left of the old garments.
The fewer and older priests
face us robed in apologies.
Shrill tailors of God's message.
Costumed nuns have died away
replaced by off-the-rack laity.

The churning suits and dresses
that draped across the pews
have worn thin and sparse.
Churches are cast off
like Good Will overcoats.
And strictures are raggedly observed.


Yet some of us still wear faith,
displaying hand-me-downs in a church
no longer fashionable.
We're not dressed as we were,
and unsure of holy style,
but hopeful of our future ensemble.

# Take It All Off

Curious that I can't laugh at myself
without also crying a little.
The foible that generates the laugh
was once a venerated bias,
social illusion I had clung to,
action I knew was significant,
reciprocal acceptance of flaw,
a fairy tale taught early to me,
mind hair that smarted when tweezed out.

And how naked I felt just after,
clutching for another fig leaf
to better hide my uncertainty,
to shield my psychic manhood from probes,
to think I had reached the New Truth
only to discern the new foible
and have to laugh again at myself.
Life consists of undressing enough
to acquire a spiritual tan.

## Ice Out

Winter lets go of the river
with parting waves of snow
and growling goodbyes
as jumbled slabs of ice,
piled shore to shore,
grind stream-grass into confetti
and toted boles of trees
drift on gelid voyages
into flotsam diaspora.

## Interlude

The small being sleeps on my chest.
My breathing sways plump arms.
He unable, me unwilling to rise and part.
We will never be closer than this touching
that he will not remember
and I will not forget.
Total unconcern nestled into gentle custody.
Neither knowing, or just now caring
about changes to come.

# Keeping Company

A woman I love
too much to hide from
has incurable cancer
flowing through her veins.

I offer what I can,
touch and presence,
while she begins to shed
what had seemed important.

We talk of others loved
and of shared absurdities
so we can avoid broaching
in harsh certainty.

She cries sometimes
to an audience of one,
not because she's dying,
but because she's losing life.

# Defining the Species

We're toolmakers and animal tamers,
dreamers and builders
and lovers and haters.
But most of all we're hedonists.

Animals cleanse themselves by
tongue-licking and mud-wallowing.
We indulge in saunas,
exfoliants and herbal douches.

The lion ignores sex
until mating during estrous.
We attempt diurnal passion
and gratuitous flirting.

The dog owns nothing
and seeks out scraps.
We amass the useless and
clamor for concocted tastes.

Our cousins the chimps
pick lice off each other.
We have life coaches
and wellness trainers.

We should wonder
if we've really accomplished
much of significance
other than indulgence.

# The Shoal

The shoal sour dries in wind drifts
as the leavings of the ebb come into view.
Shell piles here, sand there, rimmed by
barnacle rocks and wet-rotting weed.

Gulls and terns pick at scattered
remnants of crab and fish,
and lift dying clams high enough
to drop them onto the rocks.

The water almost, almost stops,
a hovering quiver in the shoal's edges,
before the surge rewets the gasping buried
on its slithering way across the crest.

Those who ignore this ever-change
are trapped by it.
One or two boats a year aground,
one or two men a decade drowned.

Feeding and dying quicken with the flow,
little fish pushed across the shoal
toward waiting jaws,
birds swooping for the crippled.

Force of water rules the shoal,
which heaves its crests and shallows
to appease the ever-flowing god
who never looks back.

The water climbs man-high above the shoal,
and, stirred only by wind,
fondles fish and weed and shell
until ebbing into turmoil.

# The Deer Chase

The dog has jumped a deer
and crashed into the woods.
He did the same a week ago
and drove the doe just past my arms,
with glance to say I'd missed.
I give no yell or whistle
to call him back to heel
for hunting is his freedom
though he's never caught a deer.
The thickets block all sight and sound
of hurtling, furry shapes, and so
I wait in silent dusk for him
to trot, all burrs and pants,
in toward the useless man,
who cannot join the chase.

# Careful Wonder

A decade ago
a friend told me
he'd killed another man.
Partly for hate
and partly from rage.
He was never caught.

He said this with reflection,
like describing a video
of his birthday party.
He told in confidence,
a confidence I've kept.
For he's a friend of a sort
truer than many.

He's caring and diligent
and speaks in quiet tones.
The beast that tore at him
slumbers.
But in meeting strangers I wonder
if they, too, can extinguish.

# The Game

I watched a baseball game last night
Played on garbage.
Strips of sod and chalked lines
Laid on thirty years of refuse.
Ephemeral movements on slow decay.
Artificial rules on artificial earth.
Winning and losing on discarded experiences.
No one noticed.

# Damn Dog Died

Damn Dog Died.
Twelve years feeding and walking together.
Seeking touches from each other.
Well-spoken, wordless glances.
Dance partners slowing in rhythm.
Damn Dog Died.

# The Yard Party

Evening breezes swirl the voices
through my open windows,
dusk-swaddled neighbors talking,
their syllables riding the air to me,
the words slurred by drink and distance,
but the emotions sounding through.

Their feelings dance behind
their masqueraded phrases,
the notes faintly shrill,
with minor chord stresses
that plead for reassurance
all is as it should be.

The voices dwindle into silence
as my neighbors detach.
Nothing said was quite a lie
nor quite the truth,
but only word-wrappings
for their hints of need.

# Taking a Pheasant

A motionless dog
thrumming wing beats
quick mount and swing
a shotgun blast
and silent echoes.

The wings crumple
and the bird drops.
A vanished focus
in a painting
brushed on air.

The odors of gun oil
of burnt powder
of cold morning sweat
drift in aromas of corn husks
and autumn earth.

The bird is dying
as the dog brings it in.
The man clasps rustling feathers
and with apology
wrings its neck.

While in his hand
the bird is breasted out.
The knife slips
and he licks his finger
tasting mingled rusts and musks.

The kill is skilled
and grants completeness
in an incomplete world
binding death together
with satisfaction.

The pheasant has provided
pride and food
for that night
and is honored in silence
for its passage.

# Revisitations

My life's settings are kept in memory
and rarely traveled back to.
For what I remember of the places
where I grew or deformed
resonates truer than a reviewing.

The cocoons I spun to live in
softened my world view
and cushioned my encounters.
The houses and cottages of my life
are furnished in memoriam

If I do revisit a former home
it is diminished and alien,
for what I valued of it left with me,
and those who shared my residence
are altered or departed.

# The Adoration

There is a secret god I worship
The abomination of light and air.
She is the manna of known gods
Of lust and war and greed.
I genuflect before her
Tithing my hate and envy.
My adoration of her scarred face
Puckers me wizened and sour.
And I would flee her temple
Of acrid incense and unholy water
But do not know where to seek
The god who lives in her absence.

# Rock Piles

When I used to hunt for deer
I'd park on a gravel road
and hike in a half-mile
on a rusty railroad track.
At a leaning swamp oak
I'd veer into the woods and
brush burrow over a ridge,
to where two deer trails
meandered across each other.

I'd set my folding stool
between two large boulders
with a tree obscured view
of the intersection
and wait.
The deer paths cut through
a long-abandoned farmstead.
A toppling chimney and stone fences
were all that remained.
Most of the stones had
found their way
back to earth
but the pattern abided.

The deer never came.
I'd spent several evenings
watching the light wane
on a monument
that carried no recollection.
The aching hand work,
gathering and stacking rocks
to clear a spot to plow
was for abandoned purpose.
And I'd been relieved
that my presence was transient
and that when I left
there would be no evidence.

# The Charter Boats

The boats string along the seam
of green and blue waters,
white mites on a fish vein,
trailing thin proboscides
that must be bitten to succeed.

The fish forage with the tides,
but sports angle by charter clock,
spending a deckhand's weekly wages
for often empty hours,
staring wistfully at shore bathers
who glance back at them as scenery.

And beneath the boats, detected
stripers and blues cruise with
closed jaws past inopportune offerings,
biding for their unfathomed time
to dine.

## Rules

The rules change at night
When coyotes prowl the gardens
And walled-in huddlers cringe
At shattered panes of glass.
No one steps into darkness
To answer dying animal cries
Or the screams of the stranded.
The rules change at night.


## Being Ignored

It's sometimes refreshing to be ignored.
When coupled horseshoe crabs hold fast against waders' feet.
When Virginia Creeper surges over mowed grass.
When young rabbits stare back without fear.
When cats in heat jailbreak to waiting lovers.
When salmon jump dams to spray their milt.
When I'm irrelevant to the process.
Tell me again how important we are.

## Storm Tossed

If the ocean would just settle down
I could read my stars and navigate.
If the ocean would just settle down
I could set out lines to catch my fate.
If the ocean would just settle down
I could swim far enough to mate.
If the ocean would just settle down
I could surface before I stagnate.
If the ocean would just settle down
I could let my self animate.

## Leaf Fall

On still days after a frost
leaves drop in dainty swirls,
curled in fatal fetal posture
and clothed in stripper's dress.
Each alone in silent parting
ignores its dormant parent
and the fall of brethren,
in post mortem passage
without burial.

# Fellow Traveler

I abide in you, too placid to wonder,
Burdened by carrying me while wallowing,
And fearing what you do not face.
You scream only when the blades snick,
When I clutch the bunched grass and weed
Of your life as I shear it.

I shun you who absorb the pain,
Knowing of my presence
But nimbly living without my weight.
I shun the sear of you who live too hot
Until with trembling hands
I enfold your sheaf and mourn.

# Noel

Amalgamated emotions, like good wine,
blendings for intensified taste.
Christmas stirrings of affection, greed and piety,
great nose, rich savor, but bittersweet aftertaste.

# Resolutions

New Year's resolutions
are meant to be broken
as soon as we realize
that deprivation and muscle strain
are not our natural state,
and that a comforted body
yields placidity of mind.

# An Apology for Hate

Unloved things—weeds and warts,
dry rot and wet rot and wall mold,
rats and lice and cockroaches
halitosis and cancer and herpes
are with us despite every effort.

But our most pernicious consort,
born of fear, reared in animosity
is hatred—of others, of change,
hate that proverbs and strictures
fumble helplessly against.

Many-splendored hate is of all sides:
radical/ reactionary, Godless/ Godfearing,
freeloving/abstinent, sharing/selfish.
It flourishes despite agonized exterminators,
an eye we refuse to pluck out.

## Stirrings

Something stirs inside my walls at night.
Rustling Creature sounds.
Is it my demented listening,
Or bugs or birds or rats?
I cannot wait for certainty,
And poison the linings of my living space.
Never knowing what was or could have been.

## Trapped Under the Yule Log

This pagan feast with Christian sauce
sets a table of colored lights
on barren winter ground
and lets us imagine
for a few unwrapped moments
that a gift can replace
unprovided caring.

# The Dog Walk

While my shepherd was alive
I walked with him late at night,
evading streetlights and lit-up houses.
Rarely met human or dog
so no leash, no words spoken.

My neighbors had all turned inward
leaving the shadows to outliers, cops,
and the creatures that hid by day.
My senses strained outward
into the dark almost silence

We held close as we prowled,
near enough that I knew
when his keener senses picked up
the yowls of possum prey
or the flicker motion of deer.

Once a feral dog chased our scent,
half again burlier than a coyote.
It moved in snarling, and we snarled back.
It sheared away, leaving us
with our share of the night.

# The Name Cascade

The same names percolate through a family like a roof leak.
And except for the Juniors and Seniors no outsiders notice.

My mother's father was Edward Willman
He had five daughters, so his name died.
Almost.

After what I suspect was an argument,
My first and middle names became
Edward Willman.

I have a cousin whose middle name
Is also Willman, without Edward.
Probably a compromise.

Family memory seems to die away
In three modern generations
But I balked.

So our infant son was given
A middle name you'll guess.
A loving infliction.

Our son called when his son arrived.
And said the middle name was Willman.
The grandfathers are pleased.

# Falling Away

Love is stepped cliffs
Of willingness to suffer.
Sheer drops from obsession to indifference.
The tiny mesa top holds less than a score
For whom I would give up my self.
Then a free fall to friends and relatives
Who are given affection and time
And a precipice further down
Acquaintances are doled out words.
And at chasm bottom are strangers
Who receive pro forma prayers and grudged money.
It's impossible to love all of humanity
When I barely like myself.

# Solitary Nocturne

As clouds shutter the night sky
and the neighbor's light is off
and the woods wear textured black,
there's no help in looking outwards.

Those alone suckle their devices
and pray for undying power,
for if heat and light vanish
there's no comfort in a candle.

Things edge closer in the blindness
and soothing lies are needed,
and someone else's breath,
there's no relief in solitary fear.

Photo credit: Hannah Edgman

# The Swamp Oak

Balding leafage
lets the eye slip through
to scabrous bark
that runs past rot holes
hiding squirrels.

Twisted branches
contort around power lines,
reaching upward
and straining to
recover grace.

The tree sways
toward a century
it will not reach,
and strews its seeds
with wanton hope.

# A Movement in the Shadows

Is that you twirling shadows
in the corner of my room?
Are you waiting for my guilt
to congeal into rank fear?
Are you blotting out the lamplight
and my hope for shards of peace?
Is your hate so strong in death
that it destroys my sleep?
Am I cursed to feel your presence
in all solitary moods?
Is it just to damn the living
for what cannot be undone?

## Commiserating Poetry Month

Our poetic anomie loves company.
We few, we sensitive, we word-obsessed,
group-clotting to read our poetry,
webzine-lurking as if in house arrest.
Always unpublished, unpaid or ego-hungry.
All but kid verse without request.
Cringing through bad verse symphonies.
Medicated so not to be depressed
when other poets miss our subtlety
and leave our tender psyches stressed.

## The Crone Zone

Never, ever cross a crone.
For if you do, she'll make you groan.
Hurry to disown your sown
Lest she intone and make you moan.
They're known, crones, for breaking bones.
And God help you, thrower of a stone,
She'll drone a curse ere you atone.
Her evil cyclone, flown to you alone
And blown across your gravestone.

# Fright of Passage

Of the unavoidable insults I undergo,
airline flights annoy me most.
Delays, discomfort and trapped disease
provided at increasing cost
without even an 'I survived' sticker.

The clitorectomy of travel enjoyment
began decades ago with shrinking seats,
security delays, luggage restrictions
and the removal of amenities and food.
I'm diminished by each transit endured.

Unlike auto independence and leisured trains
planes push me into a Venturi nozzle
that squeezes out civility and comfort
and leaves me wondering
if the destination is worth the ride.

# A Measure of Man

I reflect that which I despise.
Mourn the things not done.
Echo the words unsaid.

Falter before it's necessary.
Comprehend less than I claim.
Love through puffy self-image.

My missings are my measurements.
My flaws are my facets.
My aberrations are my absolutes.

But I am content
To stumble on, blear-sighted
In hopes of better vision.

# Currents

Moving waters scour my absurd
and point me, fish-like, into their flows.
I sumo wrestle for balance
in thick-muscled currents whose hiss
drowns out distractions,
and deaf and teetering
I find poise.

Their still moments are dreamless sleep,
my limpid wallow,
but I rouse when they waken
and surge into travel.

Salt waters churn in place,
waves featurelessly unique
that plunge onto land
in mourning for rivers' ends.
I cling to sand strips,
glimpsing brackish afterbirth
as the salt foam flicker-shifts
into the rain and rivulets
that again will course through me.

# Bedtime Story

Be careful when you wake
In the hours after midnight
For you have ebbed and the night surges.

Be careful if you wander
Into different-seeming rooms
For the other things that prowl.

Be careful of the noise in darkness,
In the creaks and cracks and rattles
For not all menace holds its tongue.

Be careful, oh be careful
In stepping from your bed
For what you fear has come.

# The Alms of Strangers

The clutching for love,
the donations from friends,
the webbing of acquaintance,
the presence of mourners.
All are sensed,
and gratitude professed.
Like tips in a diner.

Reflex affection, soul offerings
for life sustenance
and image food.
But whole lives are digested
without sensing that
gratitude can only be tasted
because of the alms of strangers.

The go-ahead allowance,
the door kept open,
the theft not committed,
the louder voice for deafness,
the tolerance of oddity,
the slander not smirched,
the nameless help offered.

When standing on the backs
of unremembered strangers,
unthinking and unthankful,
there is the height of vision
to see the things
and people
we believe are meaningful.

## Seasonal Lament

Autumn scurries past me
unnoticed,
Tints of year
unseen.
My season dissipates
Negligently,
Founders as light lessens.

## Chance Encounters

Shiny pebbles in the stream,
appealing flickers in the flow.
Never knelt to wet my knees,
and let them tumble away.
Agate and quartz, gneiss and amber,
untouched, unknown and memorable.
We seldom even spoke.

# The Sparrow Nest

The egg-fat sparrow
squats in the gutter-end
under my eave.
Brown and dirty beige,
soft chirping and stoic.

The gutter's held nests
for fourteen years
and sparrows live but five.
A granddaughter stares back,
wondering why my hatchlings
never returned to brood.

I refuse to yank the nests
or tack on mesh
despite communion wafer guano.
We're in residence
the egg-fat bird and I.

# The Predators

My fears crouch in hiding
just beyond my senses.
Creeping through the thicket
in slow and certain stalks.
No use to run and hide
or propose another victim.
The prey has been selected
and they'll charge as I falter.

To deny them is a folly,
to embrace them is a sin.
So I wait for them to pounce,
and know my listless grazing
just incites the beasts.

# The Wayfarer

The waking's spun with webs of urgent lure
And sleep is shriveled dreaming marred by fear.
The life allows the walker nothing sure
Or level path to others once held dear.
But many grasp at getting days with hope
And moments still and without vice and shame.
A little space to reassess and cope,
A quiet calm of mind, a gentle flame.
Yet many cast themselves aside and rot
And wave away this chance to reemerge.
The winnowing is fine, the chances not,
For those who see themselves as lost and purged.
The way is narrow, dimly lit and rough
But offers passage clear and good enough.

# Firelight

The allure of an open fire,
warmth aside,
is an inarticulate wish
for pyromancy,
for the flames to reveal
in flickers
the whys and wherefores
of living.
Thoughts swirl in updrafts,
grasping for
the random patterns,
tantalized
by closeness to ineffable
substance.

Photo credit: Kirsten ter Borg

# Legacy

The shuffling feet of those ahead
tramp a dust-clouded pathway
in which I just see and touch
the backs of those still living
and hear the wind-blown murmurs
of those gone further beyond.

The ever-fainter bobbing heads
have concocted my making
and conditioned my soul.
No matter how I turn
or twist away from them
their march is ever before me.

For will it or not
I am always of them,
swaddled by ancestors
who mostly know me not,
staring ahead as they shuffle on,
never looking back.

Poems from *Irregular Images* were first published in *Allegro Poetry Magazine, Ariel Chart, The Asses of Parnassus, Between These Shores Literary & Arts Annual, Bewildering Stories, Blood & Bourbon, Caesura 2017 Ascent/Descent, Chaleur Magazine, Chiron Review, Communicators League, Folk Horror Revival: Corpse Roads, The Dawntreader, Deep Waters, Dime Show Review, Dirty Chai Mag, Ealin, Encircle Publications, Eternal Remedy (ETRE), The Fat Damsel, Firefly Magazine, Garfield Lake Review, Gathering Storm Magazine, Gold Dust Magazine, Grievous Angel, Hedge Apple, Heirloom Zine, The Ibis Head Review, Imperfect Paths: Creative Talents Unleashed, Jellyfish Whispers, Light Magazine, The Literary Hatchet, Long Story Short: A Magazine for Writers, Longshot Island, LUMMOX, Medusa's Laugh Press, Metaphor Magazine, Micropoetry, Military Experience & The Arts, The MOON magazine, Nature Writing, New Pop Lit, Poems-For-All, Primal Elements, Poetry Quarterly, The Quiet Circle Magazine, Red Eft Review, Red Fez, Ricky's Back Yard, The Rising Phoenix Review, The Road Not Taken: A Journal of Formal Poetry, Samsara: The Magazine of Suffering, Sarasvati, Scarlet Leaf Review, Short Humor, Sirens Call Publications, Society of Classical Poets, Star\*Line, Tell-Tale Magazine, Inklings: Undergrad Lit & Art Magazine, Terror House Magazine, Tessellate Magazine, The Write Launch, Two Drops of Ink: A Literary Blog, Unscooped Bagel,* and *The Zodiac Review.*

# About the Poet

Edward Ahern sometimes detours into literary fiction, but he's best known as a poet and innovative genre writer. He's tucked away several awards and honorable mentions for over two hundred poems and stories and four books. The poems and stories have appeared in a dozen countries and, counting reprints, over three hundred publications. His stories can be listened to through Audible. Ed started writing fiction at sixty-seven, and poetry at seventy.

His editorial skills are based on a degree in journalism from the University of Illinois and extensive experience at the *Providence Journal*. Ed's been honing the skills for several years at *Bewildering Stories*, where he serves on the review board and as review editor with a staff of five. (*Bewildering Stories* is widely known for the author-friendly quality of its critiques.) Ed also is a member of several writing groups, including the Fairfield Scribes, where he's known for his tough-love comments.

He has his original wife, but advises that after more than fifty years together they are both out of warranty. Two children and five grandchildren serve as affection focus and money drain.

His work career after university has been an enjoyably demented hopscotch game. U.S. Navy officer (diver and bomb disarmer); reporter for the *Providence Journal*; intelligence officer living in Germany and Japan; international sales and marketing executive at a Canadian paper company (twenty-three years, seventy four countries visited, MBA from NYU); same job for the company that also owns the New England Patriots; and retirement into writing like hell to make up for lost time.

www.ingramcontent.com/pod-product-compliance
Lightning Source LLC
Chambersburg PA
CBHW031404040426
42444CB00005B/410